DO YOU KNOW

?

MUMMIES

KT-404-419

HELEN GREATHEAD

C555020707

Scholastic Children's Books,
Euston House, 24 Eversholt Street,
London NW1 1DB, UK

A division of Scholastic Ltd
London ~ New York ~ Toronto ~ Sydney ~ Auckland
Mexico City ~ New Delhi ~ Hong Kong

Published in the UK by Scholastic Ltd, 2011

Text © Helen Greathead, 2011
Illustrations © Tom Connell, 2011

All rights reserved

ISBN 978 1407 12186 4

Printed and bound in the UK by CPI Bookmarque, Croydon, Surrey

2 4 6 8 10 9 7 5 3 1

The right of Helen Greathead and Tom Connell to be identified as the author and
illustrator of this work respectively has been asserted by them in accordance with
the Copyright, Designs and Patents Act, 1988.

DO YOU KNOW...

- the weirdest ways to make a mummy?

- which mummy has the best hairdo?

- why the Egyptians wrapped their mummies up in bandages?

No? Then keep reading and you'll soon find out...

What Are Mummies?

Normally, when somebody dies, their body starts to decay, or rot away. All that is left in the end is the skeleton. But mummies are bodies that haven't decayed. Instead the soft parts are 'preserved'. The body dries up, but the skin, hair, nails and even the organs inside the body (like the heart and lungs) might still be in place.

• Sometimes people or animals are made into mummies by accident.

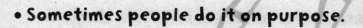

• Sometimes people do it on purpose.

THE TOP 5

Strange Places to Find a Mummy

Mummies can be hidden away undiscovered for years. When they do turn up it is often a big surprise! Mummies have been found:

5. At the top of a volcano in Peru. The mummy of Juanita the Ice Maiden was uncovered after an eruption.

4. Under a pile of rubbish. People searched and searched for Tutankhamen's tomb. It was hidden behind a pile of tomb-builder's rubbish!

3. Beneath a primary school playground. This is where archaeologists found the famous 'mummy bundles' of Peru.

2. On a building site. One Chinese mummy was accidentally chopped in half by a bulldozer when a new road was being built.

1. In a German museum – 20 mummies (and some mummified heads) were found in a box that had been mislabelled. Everyone thought the mummies had been destroyed during the war!

NEW PENS

The BEST preserved human body...

... is a natural ice mummy, nicknamed 'la Doncella', which means, the maiden. Although she died a 15-year-old girl, she is now a 500-year-old mummy! By looking at her hair and taking samples from her body, experts have worked out what la Doncella ate before she died, and even when she had her last haircut!

The WORST preserved human body...

... is a natural mummy, too. This bog body has a tricky nickname — he's called Emmer-Erfscheidenveen

Man, after the place where he was found. He is so badly preserved that experts can't be sure he's even a man! All that is left of his body is a tiny bone from his throat and one from his foot. So why do we know about him? It's because of his woolly underpants! Along with the rest of his clothes, they survived in the bog for over 3,000 years!

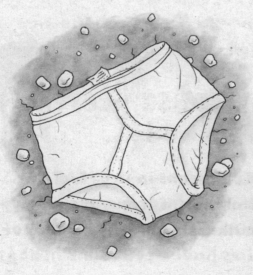

THE TOP 4

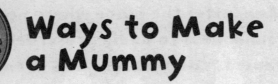

Ways to Make a Mummy

4. Early Egyptians wrapped their dead in goatskins and buried them in a pit in the DESERT SAND. The dry desert air and the hot sand quickly dried out the bodies. These first Egyptian mummies were made naturally.

3. Conditions in the PEAT BOGS of Northern Europe are just right to make mummies. Hundreds of bodies have been found in bogs.

2. Many animals and people have been preserved in ICE. If a person dies in freezing cold temperatures, ice crystals will form in the tissues of the body. Because the water in the body stops moving, the body stops decaying. The body will be preserved as long as it stays frozen.

1. Lots of ancient societies made their own mummies ON PURPOSE. But the most famous mummy-makers of all were the ancient Egyptians...

M👁️king a Mummy
ANCIENT-EGYPTIAN STYLE

Mummy-making is also called embalming or mummification. It was mostly intended for royal or very rich people. Here's how they were embalmed:

1. The dead body is placed on a sloping table. An embalmer breaks its nose. He pushes a hook up through one nostril and scoops out the brain – in bits!

2. The head is then packed with linen to help keep its shape.

3. A man called 'the slitter' cuts open the left side of the body. He pulls out the liver, the lungs, the intestines and the stomach. Each of these organs is kept in a jar called a Canopic jar.

Do You Know?

The ancient Egyptians believed that the heart was where people did all their thinking. They thought it was the most important part of the body.

They also believed that the brain was useless and should be thrown away after death!

4. The embalmers put the body in a bath filled with a type of salt called natron. This will soak up the liquid in the body. They leave the body to dry out for 40 days.

5. After 40 days the body is cleaned and rubbed with nice-smelling plant saps, called resins. It is padded out with linen, natron and sawdust, to help keep its shape. The cuts are then sewn up.

6. Next the body is decorated to make it look its best.

7. At last, the body is wrapped up to keep everything in place. Strips of linen are used for the wrapping. They hold the body together and keep nibbling insects out! There might be up to 20 layers. Linen is expensive, so sometimes old sheets, clothes and towels are used instead.

ITEMS OF JEWELLERY, CALLED AMULETS, ARE PUT BETWEEN THE LAYERS TO HELP PROTECT THE BODY FROM EVIL SPIRITS.

8. If the body belongs to someone very special, a death mask might be added. Royal mummies sometimes have gold finger and toecaps, too!

Dead-Body Beauty Tips

4. Put painted onions where the eyeballs used to be.

3. Cover the tongue with gold leaf.

2. Pop on a wig.

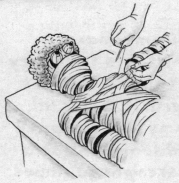

1. Stitch on a spare arm or leg, if one is missing!

Looking Inside a Mummy

Scientists have used X-rays to look inside mummies for over 100 years! They can even use a process called radiocarbon dating to find out how old a mummy is. Hair samples can reveal whether a mummy ate meat. Now a machine, called a CT scanner, can take pictures that slice right through the middle of a mummy!

DO YOU KNOW?

Some mummy-makers made mistakes that they thought they would get away with it. After all, the mummy was wrapped in linen and sealed inside a coffin called a sarcophagus. How would anyone ever know?

They had no idea that, 2,800 years later, a CT scanner would take pictures inside the linen wrappings. Now we know that a bowl of resin got stuck to a mummy's head by accident. It is still stuck fast today!

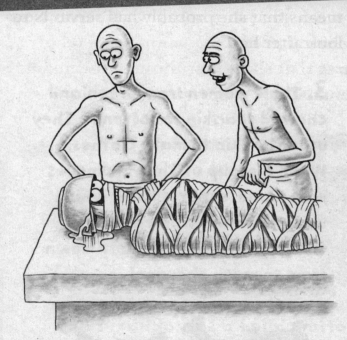

Being dead has never stopped mummies from telling us all about themselves...

THE TOP 4

Telltale Mummy Facts

4. One mummy found in the Chinese desert had super-long fingernails. With nails like that she could not work. This means that she probably had servants to look after her!

3. Thule women from Greenland chewed sealskin to soften it. They used the skin to make clothes. When a group of Thule mummies was found, experts knew which were the older women because their teeth had been worn down from so much chewing!

2. Hard skin on the feet of El Plomo Boy – an ice mummy from Chile – tell us that he had walked a very long way before he died on the top of a mountain.

1. Experts found out what Tollund Man (a bog body) had for his last supper by looking in his tummy. It was a kind of porridge made from different sorts of seeds. The seeds even tell us what season of the year he died in!

Mummies can often let us know exactly how they died...

The Secret Killer

Over 160 years ago, Sir John
Franklin and his crew sailed
two ships from England
through the freezing waters of Baffin Bay,
off the coast of Greenland.

They were searching for a quick route to
China. Their ships carried all the most modern
equipment as well as 8,000 tins of food!

The ships disappeared. Later, search parties
found three dead crewmen buried in the ice.

The bodies were examined 140 years after the ships set sail. The three men had been mummified by the ice. The researchers took samples of bone, body tissue, organs, hair and nails. They also picked up empty food tins lying near where the bodies were found.

They found that the men had lead poisoning! The lead came from the food tins. The whole crew had eaten from the tins. Lead in the body can confuse your brain and make a person weak. The tins probably helped kill the whole crew!

Bodies In the Bog

Peat is made of rotting leaves and plants. It is usually found in soggy, marshy ground – or bogs – and it lies very deep. People have cut peat out of the ground and dried it to burn for warmth for thousands of years.

But sometimes the peat cutters got a nasty surprise, because the bogs aren't only good at making fuel – they are also very good at preserving things.

Sometimes they even preserve bodies. These natural mummies are known as bog bodies.

The Making of a Bog Body

• It is winter. Somebody falls into the bog – or maybe they are pushed! The body sinks down and settles deep under the water.

• **Peat-bog water is special. It stays fresh for longer than other sources of water and it is cool.**

• A layer of moss on top of the bog seems to stop bacteria from eating away at the body and making it decay.

• **The water is still. It isn't bothered by rain, wind, snow or storms, so the body in the bog does not move.**

• Over time, however, the bog might dissolve the bones, or make them really bendy. It will make skin thick, shrivelled and leathery and give it a deep, dark tan.

Do You Know?

Bogs can change hair colour too. One bog body is nicknamed Red Franz because his beard, hair and eyebrows were dyed bright orange by the bog!

Nasty Bog Facts

Bodies found in bogs were often victims of murder!

4. Some bodies were found with a rope tied round the neck. The victim had been strangled.

3. Some had horrible head wounds. They had been bashed to death.

2. Some bodies had weights tied to them to make sure they drowned in the bog water.

1. Nobody knows why so many bodies ended up in bogs. Many of the bodies are around 2,000 years old. Experts think that the Celtic people, who lived around the bogs at that time, believed that their gods lived in the bogs. Perhaps the Celts threw people in as offerings to their gods?

Some mummies still have fingerprints. Some still have their fingernails and toenails. Lots of mummies still have very interesting hair!

THE TOP 5 Hairy Mummy Facts...

5. Chinchorro mummies, from Chile, were buried wearing wigs made from real human hair.

4. The oldest Egyptian mummy in the world used a dye called henna to cover up her grey hair. She also had extensions of real hair tied to her own hair in a fancy knot!

3. One Chinese mummy was found with head lice on her hair and nits in her eyebrows and eyelashes!

2. El Plomo Boy — from Chile — still has 200 thin plaits in his hair!

1. Clonycavan Man was dug up from a peat bog over 2,000 years after he died. His hair was still standing up in a quiff at the front. It was held up with hair gel made from pine tree resin.

The Oldest Human Mummies...

The oldest human mummy we KNOW about isn't this one...

Ötzi the Iceman is a natural ice mummy who was found high up in the Alps between Austria and Italy. At first people thought he was a hiker who had lost his way. Then scientists worked out that he was frozen 5,300 years ago! Ötzi is the oldest mummy found in Europe.

These aren't the oldest human mummies in the world either...

Three man-made mummies were found in an ancient Egyptian cemetery. They were ordinary people, not royalty. Only the women in the cemetery were preserved. Parts of the bodies were padded or wrapped in linen that had been soaked in resin. Experts think these could be the first ever man-made Egyptian mummies. They are 5,700 years old!

The OLDEST MAN-MADE MUMMIES EVER FOUND were made over 1,000 years earlier. They come from Chile, in South America...

The Oldest Man-made Mummies...

They're called Chinchorro mummies, after the village where they were made. Some of them are 7,000 years old! The ancient Egyptians often saved mummification for their kings and queens. Chinchorro people mummified everybody – old, young, rich, poor.

To make mummies, the Chinchorro people:

1. Slipped the skin off the dead body and put it to one side.

2. They then took the muscles and the internal organs from the body and used sticks to hold the bones together.

3. Next, they padded the body with plants and grasses.

4. After they padded the body, they sewed the skin back on.

5. To finish their mummies, the Chinchorro painted the mummy with a thick layer of paste.

Each Chinchorro mummy has a different face painted on it. The expression on its face tells us what sort of person the mummy was when they were alive.

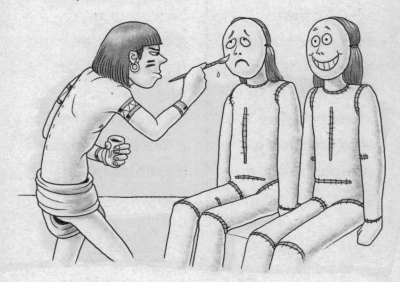

The Oldest Human Mummy EVER Found?

But which is... Well, he is known as Spirit Caveman. He comes from Nevada in the US. He was discovered about 70 years ago. At first everyone thought he was just 2,000 years old. Then, a few years ago, experts took a sample of bone and a sample of hair. They did a radiocarbon dating test and found out that the body was actually 9,400 years old!

New mummy discoveries are made every year. Maybe soon someone will find a mummy that is even older than Spirit Caveman.

Some scientists think that the early Australians may have made the first mummies. They hope to find some evidence soon!

Mummy Nicknames...

Using nicknames is an easy way to help us remember which mummy is which.

5. Ötzi the Iceman gets his name from the Ötztal Alps, between Italy and Austria, where he was found.

4. A baby mammoth mummy was found, frozen, in Siberia. She was named Lyuba after the wife of the reindeer herder who discovered her.

3. Scream-baby was found with his mouth open and traces of tears and snot on his face. Experts thought he had died horribly. The mouth often opens after death, however. He might not have been screaming at all.

2. One bog body is called Pete Marsh. It's a joke because he was found in a peat bog. D'you get it?

1. Ur-David was buried in the desert in China for 3,000 years, but he doesn't look Chinese. An American lecturer saw him and said that he thought the mummy looked just like his brother David. The name stuck! The word 'Ur' means earliest.

Why Mummy?

Nobody knows what happens when we die. So, throughout history, societies have worked out their own ideas about death. Many groups chose to mummify their dead, but not always for the same reason.

THE TOP 3

Reasons Why People Made Mummies

3. Aboriginal people in Australia used to mummify family members when they died. They didn't want their relatives to live forever, they just wanted to keep them around for longer. It helped them to grieve.

2. In Ecuador, the Jivaro Indians mummified the heads of enemies they killed. Then they boiled them down to the size of a teacup. By preserving the head they believed they would keep all of their enemies' powers!

1. Many people believe that, after death, they will carry on living in an afterlife. Ancient people made mummies look their best for this new life. They buried them with food, jewels and even servants. They believed these things would be useful in the next world.

Mummy Must-haves

Everyday things some mummies took with them to the afterlife...

A mummy found in Peru is nicknamed the Cotton King because he was wrapped in layers and layers of cotton. He was found with a catapult (for hunting in the afterlife) and a comb made from cactus spines!

The mummy of a baby found in China had a feeding bottle made from a sheep's udder buried with it. The bottle still had 3,000-year-old milk inside!

The 2,500-year-old mummy of a priestess was found buried with her make-up bag. Inside there was rouge, to colour her cheeks red, and a pointed stone used to make her eyelashes darker!

Ötzi the Iceman's clothes and equipment were made using 17 different types of tree. He carried weapons, a backpack and a fire-making kit. Some people think the moss found on his body was actually 5,000-year-old toilet paper!

Weird Ways to Make a Mummy

PINE FRESH!

A family that was buried in Hungary nearly 250 years ago was mummified by accident. They were preserved by the cool dry air in their tomb, and by their coffins! The coffins were made of pine. Oil from the wood helped to preserve the bodies.

IN IT TOGETHER!

In Peru, some Inca people were found in 'mummy bundles'. Up to seven people were wrapped up inside each one. Each of the bundles had a false head on top, to make it look like one person!

DO IT YOURSELF!

Around 3,000 years ago, some Buddhist monks in Southeast Asia tried to mummify themselves! They stopped eating certain foods and sat alone in a chamber with candles to help dry out their bodies.

The Most Famous Mummies

Horatio Nelson, was a very
famous naval admiral.
He was killed at the
Battle of Trafalgar just
over 200 years ago.
Dead sailors were
usually buried at
sea. But Nelson
was a hero!
His officers
wanted to
give him a
proper funeral.
They needed
to preserve
the body until
they could get it
back to England,

so they put their admiral in a barrel
of brandy. The alcohol in the brandy
stopped his body from decaying!

Vladimir Lenin was a hero too,
because he helped to plan the
Russian Revolution. When he
died – nearly 90 years ago
– the people of the Soviet
Union were very upset. The
government decided to
mummify Lenin's body
and put it on show. In just
three days, one million
people went to see it.

But not long before
Lenin died, Howard
Carter discovered
the tomb of...

The Most Famous Mummy Ever

Tutankhamen, or Tut for short, was made king when he was just nine years old. He died when he was about 18 and was buried in a titchy tomb. Then everyone forgot all about him.

So why is King Tutankhamen THE MOST FAMOUS MUMMY EVER?

Ancient Egyptian kings were usually buried in enormous tombs – like the pyramids. King Tutankhamen's tomb isn't very big. That's because nobody expected him to die so young. His real tomb hadn't been finished!

It was normal for tombs to be raided by robbers soon after the mummy's funeral.

King Tutankhamen's tomb was small and hidden away, so the robbers missed it. The tomb had hardly been touched since it was sealed. When Howard Carter found the tomb, most of King Tutankhamen's treasures were still inside.

As they entered, Carter and his team couldn't believe their eyes...

... there were over 3,000 treasures inside!

Things King Tut Took With Him

10. A selection of boomerangs so that Tut could hunt in the afterlife. Some were made from gold and ivory.

9. Lots of beds. One of them folded up like a camp bed!

8. Jewellery – rings, earrings, buckles and neck collars.

7. Chariots — they had been taken apart to fit inside the tomb.

6. Over 400 little statues of servants, called shabtis, who would serve Tut in the afterlife.

5. A golden throne, as well as smart chairs and stools.

4. Boats – most mummies needed one boat to take them to the afterlife, but King Tut had over 30 of them!

3. Lots of coffins — Tut's mummy was inside a solid gold coffin. The gold coffin was inside three more coffins. The coffins lay inside four gold-painted boxes. These boxes were held in a huge stone sarcophagus.

2. Fancy gold finger and toecaps – he even had golden sandals!

1. Most amazing of all was King Tut's beautiful face mask. It is made of solid gold decorated with coloured stones and glass. The mask has been in exhibitions, on posters and book covers. Lots of people recognize it. It is the mask that made the mummy of King Tutankhamen the most famous mummy EVER.

Tomb Robberies!

Ever since there have been tombs, some people have wanted to steal from them. In ancient Egypt, a robbery sometimes happened before the mummy was even buried! Priests or tomb workers helped themselves, then sealed up the tomb thinking that no one would know!

Robbers took metals that could be melted down and sold. They took food and wine. They unwrapped mummies and took the amulets in their wrappings. Sometimes they even took the linen the mummy was wrapped in!

Do You Know?

Some tomb chambers were hidden behind a maze of secret passages. It often took archaeologists years to find a way in. Often, when they found the tomb at last, it had already been robbed!

Sometimes robbers left a messy trail of bones and wrappings behind them.

Sometimes they tunnelled into a tomb really carefully. You could hardly see that they had been!

Over 2,000 years ago, in the Altai Mountains of Asia, some grave robbers set to work. They tunnelled into the tombs and stole all of the valuables. Then they ran off, leaving open their tunnel into the tomb.

Water flowed in through the tunnel and froze in the cold mountain air. The bodies were prepared for mummification, but now they would freeze in the water. The grave robbers had accidentally helped the mummies! When the tomb was discovered, over 2,000 years later, the bodies were perfectly preserved.

Mummy Tattoos

3. Ötzi the Iceman had tattoos in strange places. They were made up of lines and crosses. X-rays show that the tattoos matched parts of the body where his bones were stiff with arthritis. Maybe the tattoos were for healing?

2. Five mummies found together in Greenland had the same blue lines tattooed above their eyebrows. The tattoos showed that the mummies all belonged to the same family.

1. Two hundred years ago, the Maori people of New Zealand often had fancy tattoos on their heads – and on their bottoms! When an important person died their head would be mummified as a mark of respect.

Europeans once paid big money for Maori heads. Some are still on display in museums. Today, the Maori people believe that this is no way to treat their ancestors. They want the heads back!

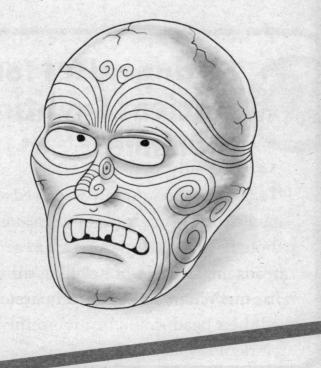

Things to Do With Mummy

Egyptian tomb robbers often didn't know what to do with all the mummies they found – there were so many of them! There had to be a way of making money from a mummy...

THE TOP 4

Strange Uses for Ancient Egyptian Mummies

4. Ground-up mummy was used as a medicine for hundreds of years. People thought it cured anything from a headache to a fear of heights! It didn't. The medicine was completely useless.

3. One businessman bought up loads of mummy bandages. He wanted to turn them into writing paper! The paper came out a dirty brown colour.

2. Artists once used ground-up mummy paste in their paintings! That also came out an interesting shade of brown!

1. Tourists to Egypt 200 years ago could pay for a trip to a tomb, pick out a mummy and have it taken back to their hotel. They could then watch as the mummy was unwrapped before their very eyes.

WHERE TO PUT UNWANTED MUMMIES

Around 150 years ago, a strange law was made in the Mexican town of Guanajuato. The law said that families with a relative in the local graveyard had to make a payment every year to keep them there. If a family couldn't afford to pay one year, their relative would be dug up again!

The gravediggers got a big shock when they had to start digging up the bodies. Because of the dry air and the type of soil they were buried in, some of the bodies had turned into mummies!

What could they do with these bodies? Simple. Put them on show in the local museum. You can still see them there today. There are 111 of them!

The Smallest Mummy...

The Guanajuato museum claims to have on show the smallest mummy in the world. It is the sad little mummy of a baby who died with its mother.

But the museum people didn't know about a type of stingless bee from Australia that mummifies beetles when they try to break into its hive! In just ten minutes the bee wraps its enemy in wax, resin and mud. The beetle dries out and turns into a mini-mummy!

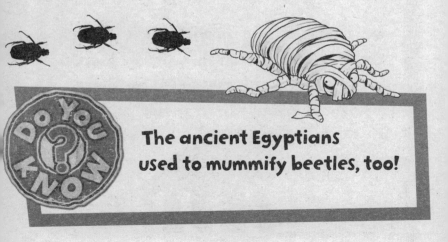

The ancient Egyptians used to mummify beetles, too!

The **Biggest** Mummy...

Only one mummified dinosaur has ever been found. It is a natural mummy of course. The dino died 67 MILLION years ago! Usually dinosaur finds are fossilized but this one still has bones, skin and body tissue! The dinosaur was a hadrosaur. Alive, it would have been around 12 metres long and weighed 3.5 tonnes! It's probably the OLDEST MUMMY EVER FOUND, too.

Ancient Egyptian Animal Mummies

The ancient Egyptians didn't just mummify people. They mummified animals too – millions of them! Dogs, cats, monkeys, gazelles, baboons ... even crocodiles!

Their god, Sobek, had the head of a crocodile. He controlled the waters of the Nile. People wanted the Nile to flood each year, because it helped them grow the food they needed. They worried that if anyone hurt a crocodile, they might upset Sobek and the floods would not come. So crocodiles were protected.

One city even had a crocodile temple. The spoiled crocs wore jewels and swam in their own special pool. Then, when they died, they were treated like royalty – and mummified.

Ancient Egyptians believed the water of the River Nile was actually Sobek's snot!

DO YOU KNOW?

Weirdest Thing Found in a Mummy's Tummy

Lyuba, the mammoth baby, was frozen in ice about 40,000 years ago. She was so well preserved that she still had eyelashes! By looking at the baby tusks that were growing inside the little mammoth, experts worked out that Lyuba had died:

- aged just one month
- in the spring
- by accident

Inside her tummy they found 40,000-year-old mammoth poo! They weren't surprised. Mammoths were very like elephants. Baby elephants eat their mothers' poo. The poo helps to prepare their tummies so that once they start eating plants they can digest them properly.

MOST MYSTERIOUS MUMMY MYSTERY – SOLVED!?

For a long time, nobody really knew how King Tut died. Experts had lots of different ideas:

- had he been poisoned?
- was it a hunting accident?
- had he been bashed on the head?

Strangely, people liked to think Tut had been murdered. It made his story more exciting.

King Tut did have a nasty bash on his head. This helped people to believe he had been murdered. They even came up with one or two suspects.

Now, some experts are spoiling everyone's fun. They believe that the blow to the head probably happened when Tut was first taken out of his tomb, around 90 years ago.

They say that King Tut wasn't murdered at all and that he broke his leg a few days before he died. The break they believe, caused an infection. The infection probably led to his death!

Spooky Mummy Stories...

Some people think stories of the bogeyman are linked to bog bodies. But the bogeyman is just a folk tale. Are any spooky mummy stories true?

TUT'S CURSE

Soon after Tut's tomb was opened, Lord Carnarvon died. Because he had helped discover the tomb, many people worried that Tut's mummy had cursed him! Some ancient Egyptian tombs did have curses written on the walls. Tut's didn't — but that didn't stop people imagining it. They claimed that terrible things happened to people who were connected with the tomb. But the story was exaggerated. Experts now know it is not true.

THE MOVING ARM...

When one tomb was opened around
130 years ago, workers found so many
mummies they had to line them up outside
the tomb for some time. Slowly, the arm of
one of the mummies really did start to lift
up! The workers were terrified!
The mummy was not coming to life. It had
grown very hot in the Egyptian sun. The
heat had melted the resins in the wrappings.
That's what made the arm move!

A Funny Way To Move A Mummy

A man named Johan Reinhard found the mummy of Juanita the Ice Maiden, at the top of one of Peru's highest mountains. The girl belonged to the Inca people. They had left her there to freeze to death, believing she was going to live with their gods.

Luckily, Reinhard is an archaeologist. He knew he had to move Juanita quickly, or the ice preserving her body would start to melt. If the ice melted, Juanita's body would decay.

The frozen mummy was very heavy. Reinhard carried her all the way down the mountain on his back. Then he put Juanita on the bus to the nearest city – Arequipa. It was nice and cool in the hold of the bus and, when Juanita arrived in the city, they popped her straight into the freezer!

Johan Reinhard is Explorer in Residence at the National Geographic Magazine. He knows a lot about mummies and how to protect them. Two hundred years ago, things were very different...

Three Early Egyptologists

Giovanni Belzoni

After Giovanni Belzoni retired from working as a circus strongman, he started collecting ancient Egyptian souvenirs for the British Consul – but he wasn't much better than a grave robber! He didn't mind trampling on a fragile mummy to get to the best treasure.

William Matthew Flinders Petrie

When he was 13, William Matthew Flinders Petrie read a book on the pyramids and decided he had to visit them. He started work in Egypt over 100 years ago – and stayed for 37 years! Petrie insisted on recording and studying everything that was found in a tomb – from broken bits of pottery to handfuls of earth!

Howard Carter

Howard Carter worked as an artist on some of Petrie's digs. He later became an archaeologist and is best known for discovering the tomb of Tutankhamen. Like Petrie, he was careful to examine everything he found in there. It took him and his helpers ten years to record it all!

Do You Know?

Early archaeologists threw away the bodies of the mummies they found and only kept the heads. They thought the head could tell them everything they needed to know about the mummy.

Mummies in Danger!

At one time there wasn't much difference between archaeologists and tomb robbers. Today, tomb robbers still cause problems. Archaeologists often have to race to reach new sites before they are disturbed. They will try to get a mummy to the safety of museum or university to study it.

But archaeologists now face a new problem, too – climate change.

Sea levels are rising — sites near the coast may be lost forever.

Temperatures are rising — frozen tombs may begin to thaw.

One good thing is that climate change might help to uncover new mummy finds. But will the archaeologists get to them in time – before the robbers take their share and before the mummies start to decay?

Let's hope so!

Mummies Quiz

1. What are mummies?

   a) bodies of people that have been murdered
   b) bodies of animals
   c) bodies that haven't decayed

2. Where was Juanita the Ice Maiden found?

   a) up a volcano
   b) in a freezer
   c) on a bus

3. How do we know about Emmer-Erfscheidenveen Man?

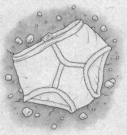

   a) from the discovery of his car
   b) from the discovery of his perfectly preserved pants
   c) from the discovery of his footprints

4. Which one of these will not preserve a body?

   a) ice
   b) desert sand
   c) stew

5. How did the Egyptians make their mummies beautiful?

   a) they put on a wig and put painted onions where their eyes once were
   b) covered the mummies in glittery tattoos
   c) dyed their hair

6. How did Sir John Franklin's crew die?

   a) they drowned
   b) they choked
   c) lead poisoning

7. What is a bog?

   a) a dirty toilet
   b) soggy or marshy ground where you can find peat
   c) a place for keeping mummies

8. Which of these items has not been found alongside a mummy?

a) a make-up bag
b) a mobile phone
c) a comb

9. How was Horatio Nelson's body preserved?

a) it was wrapped in linen and covered with resin
b) it was put in a barrel of brandy
c) it was buried in desert sand

10. Who discovered the tomb of Tutankhamen?

a) Howard Carter
b) Ötzi the Ice Man
c) Vladimir Lenin

INDEX

Also available...

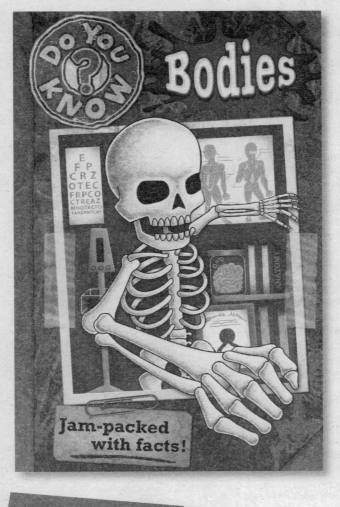

Coming Soon...

Do You Know? Extreme Wheels
Do You Know? Sharks